WITHDRAWN

AFTER THE BEGINNING

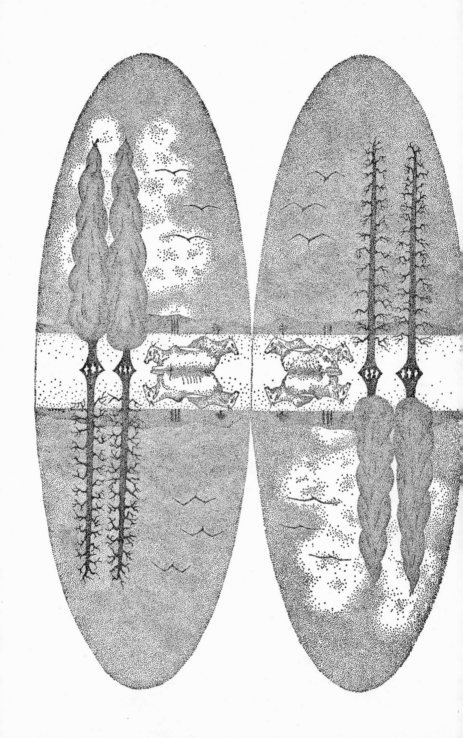

Sarah Singer

AFTER THE

BEGINNING

Dublin · New Hampshire

WILLIAM L. BAUHAN · PUBLISHER

1975

GRAMLEY LIBRARY
Salem Academy and College
Winston-Salem, N. C. 27108

PS
3569
I574
A7

Copyright © 1975 by Sarah Singer

All rights reserved. No portion of this book may be reproduced without permission of the publisher, except by a reviewer who may quote brief passages.

Library of Congress Catalog Card No. 74-78069
ISBN: 0-87233-032-X

Drawings by Rachel Singer

COMPOSED AND PRINTED IN LINOTYPE GRANJON
AT THE CABINET PRESS, INC., MILFORD, N. H., U.S.A.

For Leon

Husband, friend, critic

2-76

ACKNOWLEDGMENTS

THE LYRIC for Journey, "In the beginning was the Word", Barter, The Winding Sheet, and Skating Rink-Rockefeller Center; FIDDLEHEAD and THE DIAMOND ANTHOLOGY for The Mad Librarian; INTERNATIONAL WHO'S WHO IN POETRY ANTHOLOGY for Eve; POET LORE for After the Beginning and Suicide; YANKEE for Unquiet Flesh; NEW MEXICO QUARTERLY for Requiem; CHICAGO JEWISH FORUM for Hand-Hewn Headstone; IMPRINTS QUARTERLY for Indian Madonna, Guadalupe, Mexico, Boy in His Own Season, and Helen of Troy Twenty Years Later; QUICKSILVER for Roses Curled in Unbelief.

THE GOLDEN QUILL ANTHOLOGY for Aubade, Land Burial for One Who Drowned, "In the beginning was the Word", Indian Madonna, Boy in His Own Season, In Nomine (under the title After the Beginning), and Barter.

Apple In The Hand, Bred From Dismissal, Quarrel, In Nomine (under the title After The Beginning), Noah, and After The Odyssey appeared in THE NEW YORK TIMES. © 1956, 1957, 1963, 1970 by The New York Times Company. Reprinted by permission.

Ghetto Child is reprinted by permission from THE CHRISTIAN SCIENCE MONITOR. © 1971 The Christian Science Publishing Society. All rights reserved.

CONTENTS

[9]

III.   Goliaths with Six-Guns

IV.   Girl of Sumer

I

AFTER THE BEGINNING

GRAMLEY LIBRARY
Salem Academy and College
Winston-Salem, N. C. 27108

AFTER THE BEGINNING

CHARACTERS

Adam
Seth: son of Adam
Enosh: son of Seth
Kenan: son of Enosh, grandson of
Seth, great-grandson of Adam

SETH:

It all began that Spring. We buried Eve
And watched the awned wheat sicken, the dread shape
Of dust unspell the vineyards and bereave
Fraught bud of bounty. Dune and desertscape
Encroached upon the fields, sown substance bled
Till men grew lank, and puzzled beasts gnawed stone
For provender. All easement died, unbred
To lean-ribbed silence bleak with the unknown.
Days merged, lacklustre, umbrous dawns and dusks
Measured by want, defined in shards of rye
And blighted ephahs gleaned, in final husks
Of bitter corn; time-circled air and sky
Dyed grim as dustfall, light itself undone
To blind murk hueless as oblivion.

KENAN TO ENOSH:

'My father, what is light?' I asked. 'The sun.'
'And what are winds?' 'But restive tides of air
Quickened to leaf-wise flurry. Now have done
With questions, boy, for dazzled skies turn rare,
And rife with April meaning, furrows wait

The sowers and the seed.' 'Is sin yet clad
In apple scent? Grown vexed, does God berate?'
'You hush now, boy, lest others think you mad.'
Thus cautioned Father Enosh, prophecy
Like doom upon his tongue, foreshadowing
The child grown alien, all identity
To kind and kinsman lost; the subtle sting
Of utter singleness, the narrowed span
Of unshared self embittering the man.

KENAN:

The voices scourged. I cried upon the wind
And fled their echoing scorn, past stile and field,
Past lichened forest-places until dinned
Scurrilities unvoiced, and blue air reeled
With stillnesses. Noon-spelled, the grass was dumb
And did not sing derision. Gowned in light,
The ragwort glistened like the rose—not come,
As I, to grief—diversity its right.
Therein lay balm, therein affinity
That eased the ache of self and shaped the fret
Of mind to dream, to such serenity
As tempered grove and greensward; therein met
Disparity and wisdom, earth's intent
Toward all fruition made equivalent.

ADAM TO KENAN:

Attend me, Kenan, we are more than kin.
Proclaimed pariah who would fain divest
Horizons of their secrets, who within
The seed seek end and source, we are at best
But wearisome anomalies accorded
The thistle-pricks of scorn. We share a strange
Community, I, Adam, with my hoarded

Remembrances, and you who fathom change.
Our separate climates mingle, youth and age,
Each complement to each, on each conferred
Such exquisite perception, we grow sage
Beyond our single scope. Divergence spurred
To unison, we barter dream and wit,
Who were apart, now rendered aggregate.

ADAM TO KENAN:

Envision, Kenan, hue and gossamer
Textured to newnesses of bloom and grass,
The first-fledged wing in flight, the primal stir
Of untried winds. Envision, come to pass,
Unending sheaves, such fruitwise plenitude
As reaffirmed itself, the bud unsealed
Itself regenerate, the fruit imbued
With total sequence, yield engendering yield.
Fulfillment tempered time. There bred an ease
Upon the air, a God-loved consonance
That nurtured graces, kindred cadences
In flesh and fruit and pristine circumstance
Of clime and cloud: creation yet untaught
By cunning, and omnipotently wrought.

ADAM TO KENAN:

Here bred mortality. Strange vapors clung
To leaf and unlearned fruit. Here windflaws racked
The unapt flesh and blooming nettle stung.
Here wonted beasts, grown predatory, tracked
And blooded. Vulturous bird-things cried and rent
The alien air. Here daylight gloomed, amiss
With sudden squall. Here dwelt presentiment,
Here blasted scarp, here quagmire and abyss.
No plenty graced; no roseate balm appeased.

[15]

Death hovered, scant existence fraught with bane
And utmost plight. Here hope nor fancy eased,
For wretched herb and wildling could sustain
But merest breath. All human anguish summed
And dreads compounded, here endurance plumbed!

ADAM TO KENAN:

We shunned the light. Pernicious fever smote,
Enfeebling thew and limb,—and then, at last,
Infliction ebbed, and Eden grew remote,
Its utter prime unalterably cast
To retrospect and dream. Reality
Was stint and season, growth administered
By willful gust and weather, pod nor tree
Yet culminant, profusion yet inferred.
Tutored by need, we nurtured flock and furrow,
Urged tendril to fruition and retrieved
Barren to sward, incipience to thorough
Fecundity till stony waste achieved
Succulent issue, bean and berry hulled
And ripe with portent, harvest to be culled.

ADAM TO KENAN:

'Go cool your wits,' they hoot. 'Your tale has thinned
To dross, to graybeard fable! It may be
The wind will listen and the tamarind.'
Affliction taints them, Kenan. 'Fantasy
Will grow no corn,' they fret, 'nor grass one flock
When drouth cheats seed. Old man, your hunger spawns
Illusive groves, your Eden dreamed to mock
These stony furrows and our sterile dawns!'
Suckled on bitterweed, they chide and shun
All breadth and luminous concept, so construe
Prescribed existence, its phenomenon
Wears paucity and shade. Their meager due

But wind and desert-dearth, they starve and thrust
At shadows, Kenan, who must plow the dust.

KENAN TO ADAM:

Enough of death! Enough of beggared grove
And futile lamentation. Succour bides
Beyond those hills. I know where lustrous cove
And river beckon, and the dew resides
On rush and ungalled bough. But we must choose:
Here scrag and shroud, or exile and redress
For blight; known ways for alien; what we lose
Exchanged for gain, the greater for the less.
To falter is to perish. Dearth exhorts
The bitter boon of flight, harsh anodyne
Of challenge and displacement, end that courts
The fullness of beginning. Yours and mine
To hasten exodus, our task to shape
Bewilderment to purpose and escape.

ADAM TO KENAN:

Take comfort, Kenan. Heritage compels
Survival and perverse subsistence wrung
From scourge and pitfall. Precedence foretells
Continuing redemption. Here among
The hopeless and distraught, we must ensure
Departure, so prevision likelihood
That all may quicken to its promise—hewer
And seedsman rallied, those who scoff—withstood.
Go forth now, Kenan. Gather pristine fruit
From outland groves. Bear hither wild-bred vine
And palm yield, orchard essence to refute
Ill-omened disbelief. Who yet repine
Must soon take heart. Abundance shall persuade
The scorners, and embolden the dismayed.

DONKEY AFTER EDEN

There is no moon, and it is cold.
That other starry place
Was always warm, its air
Alight with wings.
I would race
Sweet winds and never tire,
Drink from ample springs . . .
I thirst and hunger here,
Grow old.

There are stones beneath my feet
And no grass.
Tonight there will be sleet.

Daylong am burdened now
Who bore no weight
Save garland brushed with dews
The laughing girl would plait . . .
I drag a plow;
Bit and harness bruise;
Nettles lame my gait.

Unaware,
I drowsed and fed
On wild rye and sorrel
Before we fled . . .

I hear them quarrel
Huddled by the fire.
Each blames the other

And the woman weeps.
At last they move together,
Whisper, sleep.

Driven out
That flowered afternoon,
We labor in this bitter land
Of ice and drought
Where flowers die
And battered leaves are strewn—
I do not understand
How or why.

EVE

Clothed in impeachable innocence,
Eva, plaiting her hair,
Of sin, of destined penitence
Is undulantly unaware;

Her lips, her fingers berry-stained,
Her loins white as a cloud;
Its ultimates not ascertained,
Not wise, her flesh, nor proud.

Her body's slight perimeter,
Of tranced passivity,
Not need beset, does not yet stir
With prime nativity.

Their subtleties unwarranted,
Her senses sleep untried
By human hungers not yet bred,
By scourge and fratricide.

Eve, sweet with grass and garlanded,
Indifferent of ease,
Her languorous hours a pyramid
Of small monotonies,

Insentient, and devoid of will,
Unseeking, is unsought,
With Adam's touch upon her still
As merest wind, as naught.

Undreamed is flight and flaming sword,
The wrath that shall inspire
The drumbeat pulse, its underscored
Crescendo of desire;

All genesis, its paraphrase
Of human love defined
With innocence and Eden's ways
Forever left behind.

The serpent coiled about her feet,
Eve is plaiting her hair,
As yet unmeasured by deceit,
And undulantly unaware.

IN NOMINE

*"Whatsoever Adam called every living creature,
that was the name thereof."* (Gen. II. 19)

If Adam had not named each kind,
And given it identity,
No bird nor beast would be defined
Beyond its unnamed entity

Of shape, of furred or feathered flesh
Not yet prescribed or understood:
The hawk unhawklike as the thrush,
No lion phrased to lionhood.

Creation poised, the very air
Yet unapprised of lilt and wing
Till Adam turned to them, aware,
And named the birds and beasts to being.

NOAH

Elect, he scans the look of sky,
And shapes the stubborn gopher wood
To side and keel as sea mews cry
Where land birds once found nesting good;

Where crickets hush, unlike their kind,
And leaves grow slack in air like brass.
He hammers till the days go blind,
And dooms of darkness flood the grass.

He shuns encounter. Given grace,
Apprised of heavenly intent,
He turns from each unhallowed face
Stricken with prescience, all but spent

With loss, with knowing . . . Cursed and blessed,
He herds the chosen throng aboard
While thunder trumpets east and west
The omnipresence of the Lord.

When God looked out and nothing was
Save elemental sweep
Of water governed by no laws,
And winds yet locked in sleep;

When time yet timeless held no sound
Beyond silence that was not,
And all of symmetry lay drowned,
God thought and thought and thought

Until He phrased the universe,
Divine vernacular
Evoking nightfall to rehearse
The purport of a star.

II

DANDELION CLOCKS

"SUFFER THE LITTLE CHILDREN . . ."

NEWS ITEM: Grace ————, thirty-seven years old, once
spent two years in a mental institution because she
drowned her three children in a bathtub "to keep them
safe," she said. Now, ten years later, after rearing a new
family of three, she has repeated her tragic act.

"Where are Mary, Nicholas, John,
Twice-begotten flesh and bone?
Then as now, now as then,
Water brings oblivion.

Their hands are still,
And noon's quiet ritual of light,
Yellow as a daffodil,
Endues dead limbs with grace.
Safe beyond star
And solstice, beyond dreads that lace
The night with nightmare,
And fall, and shuddering height
Upon the edge of sleep . . .
Let no one weep!

Hush, dandelion clock!
And hush, wind at my door!
What admonitions mock
Now as before?

Yesterday and long ago,
See what the mirror saw:
All imminence in stark tableau—

Fang and flame, fist and claw;
Ring-a-round and mulberry bush;
London Bridge is falling down;
Thorns to prick, stones to crush
Mary, Nicholas, and John.

Hush, dandelion clock!

But what of winds that will not cease?
(Hush, tick and tock!)
Blown leaves throng the air like geese,
The doomed hour struck!
And what of portent never done?
Yet unbegotten flesh and bone
Pricked by thorn, crushed by stone—
Water brings oblivion."

BARTER

When autumn's cool treason
Abstracts the season,

And summer's estranged
As prearranged,

How still the cicadas!
When grassy cantatas

Grow plaintive and thin
As a violin,

The lost hours struck
On the dandelion clock

Seem hurried toward night,
Yet pause to delight

In munificence proffered,
In autumnally coffered

Gold coin in rebuttal
For fragrance and petal.

GHETTO CHILD

This is his shore, and this his sea:
Street daylong parched with summer drouth,
Then flood in tideless mimicry
Out of the hydrant's iron mouth

Devoid of towering sea-sound caught
In rock-rimmed cove, in wrack-hung shell.
Perched on a curb, this Argonaut
Sails paper boats on a gutter swell.

BOY IN HIS OWN SEASON

Do not call him now.
He will not hear you
Where he stands,
Poised upon a hill,
His fledgling lankness
No less endowed with prime
Than noon-spelled leaf.

Winds possess him,
And horizons.

Summered as birds,
He dreams weightless
Metaphors of flight,
And soars upward
Toward the sun
Devoid of wings.

ROSES CURLED IN UNBELIEF

I wept, and deafer than the grass,
The day, midsummer-ridden, seemed
Enwrought by Vulcan out of brass.
Fired and still and unredeemed,

The bramble bush burned unaware.
I wept, and nothing understood,
Not dandelions with yellow hair,
Nor thistle beard nor arrowwood

That all the morning dews were blind,
That roses curled in unbelief.
I wept, my childhood left behind
In that immoderate grief.

"GREEN AND DYING"* IN 8 MILLIMETER FILM

It is summer where you walk
Through fields that never know decline,
Trail butterfly, touch leaf and stalk.

Aware of camera eye, you gawk
And giggle, posture by design.
It is summer where you walk.

Your shoes discarded, canter, balk,
Kick over traces that confine,
Trail butterfly, touch leaf and stalk.

By turns grow still or full of talk
Of birthday presents. You are nine.
It is summer where you walk.

Just out of range, what circling hawk?
Child, on screen, yet sunned benign,
Trail butterfly, touch leaf and stalk.

Old reels unwind to mock, to mock
With portent love could not divine.
It is summer where you walk,
Trail butterfly, touch leaf and stalk.

*From *Fern Hill* by Dylan Thomas

OLD WOMAN AND HOUSEPLANT

She speaks to it, feeds it love
Bright as water; mulches soil,
Looks with anxious eyes for proof
Of growth; its windowed aureole

Of bloom her bit of garden coaxed
From seed to witness going, coming,
Greet her waking with its fixed
Season, clay-pot summer flooding

Her shadowed room with light. Spared
Jar of weather, blossom seethes.
Born of her nurture, in their shared
Refuge, she almost hears it breathe.

PARK PLAYGROUND

Daylong we watch as they become
Strangers who greet tortoise, hare,
Child-high steed; beguiled in realm
We cannot enter, light like water

Glossed upon fledgling limb and throat.
As slides are braved, stone horses groomed,
We bide our time, anticipate
Play's aftermath and kinship claimed

Anew; our tired adventurers
Come home for now while we who mind
Their needs rejoice. What prescience stirs
Unheeded as we soothe, feed, bind?

HAND-HEWN HEADSTONE

No stranger's hand inscribed this stone,
This epitaph for graced flesh, bone

That once was Jonathan whose ways
Made summits of his mother's days,

And leafed his father's waking air.
Whose footfalls rocked the silent stair,

Whose uttered name belled wind and sky,
Now lettered mute where hushes lie,

And dews are sorrows filigreeing
This stony sequel to unbeing.

BRED FROM DISMISSAL

I shall become
Sealed in death, dumb;

What summary known
Recorded in stone;

Grass over me
As a green sea;

Roots thrust under
To suck, to plunder,

To nourish their kin
On what has been;

To breed from dismissal
Wild rye and thistle.

FOR JACK AND RACHEL
WHO WERE ONCE LOST

Where are they,
The children lost in the woods?

Only the stricken leaves answer
While streams mock the color of eyes,
And toadstools taint
Uttered names.

Nothing.
Detritus of dead seasons
And lichens' silken onslaught
Upon stones.

Yield them up, woods, before night
Nails moth and hoot owl to trees.
We are waiting with bread
And candles.

IDIOT BOY

He watched from the sidelines,
Melon head bobbing,
Limbs askew.

    Take a giant step,
    Ring-a-leavio,
    Hide, seek—

Idiot eyes followed.

We did not break his bones
With sticks and stones.
We stuck out tongues,
And bellowed epithets instead.

The slack mouth
Grinned or grimaced,
Gulped air
Like a beached fish.

DANDELIONS

They cut a swath,
Soon take over,
Yet I am loath
To root them out
Who flaunt such yellow hair,
Regale gadabout
June bug, moth;
Whose ranks parade
Daylong, somehow evade
Advancing mower,
Rear up, make free
With dew and wind.
Regret but brief
For disciplined
Once unbreached lawn,
Grown fond of weed
(Or are they flower?)
I look on
And let them be.

LANCELOT UPON A PLASTER STEED

Call it a pilgrimage,
Call it what you will,
The long way back; the child,
The man come full circle.
Here in this littered field,
Echoes rage
Upon the light, voice and footfall
Summoned into being . . .
Spun haze of August filigreeing
Remembered hue and essence . . . sprawl
Of tent and carousel;
Midway, vendor's booth,
Ferris wheel and game of chance;
The sawdust dance
Of clown and tumbling dwarf; crude barker's spiel
Purporting to be truth . . .

Ladies and gentlemen . . .
Come one, come all!
Welcome to Brady's
Carnival!

To thrill you, and chill you—
Strongman, freak;
Zulu chief
From Mozambique.

Pinhead, giant,
Tattooed lady;
Voodoo man
Direct from Haiti;

Ella, the seal girl—
Ladies and gents,
The price of admission,
Just twenty-five cents.

Listen . . . Only the wind among the weeds . . .

Turn back the year
To childhood . . . Place the carousel here,
Its gilded fantasy
Of flight and plunging hoof,
Its long ago calliope
Wrested from oblivion.
Trace the warp and woof
Of dream purchased for coin,—
The boy astride the horse become
All the knights in Christendom:
Bayard, Roland, brave of deed,
Lancelot upon a plaster steed,
Slayer of dragons beyond sum—
Dream and carousel grind on and on and on.

It is the afternoon
Of innocence. The boy
Nibbles cotton candy,
Buys a striped balloon.

Walk with him the tawdry length
Of midway. Scan huckster's shelves
And sideshow . . . All, all beguile.
Follow him through the turnstile
Into the labyrinth
Whose twisted paths to nowhere
Double back upon themselves.

Run here, run there,
Become quarry none pursues;
Turn about and about,
(Panic rising like a shout)
Cul-de-sac to confuse—
Sudden light! The way out!

Sneakered feet pause.
Encased in glass,
A waxwork gypsy stares
At all who pass
With agate eyes
Like solitaires ...
Game wheels spin;
Stakes are lost and won;
Three o'clock day
Shimmers with butterflies.
The boy, clutching tinseled prize
That will not stay
The wind, nor fall of leaf, nor sun,
Enters the darkened nickelodeon.

Flags and tent flaps droop.
The boy turns homeward, halts,
Yet locked in dream; and dreaming vaults
Over slack-tied rope
And tentpin, peers into each dim
Interior ... Wig, battered trunk ... polyglot
Sound ... canvas world where carney bum
And palmist, spieler and Hottentot,
Curse heat, dirt, flies, and tedium.

Here and now
While moth and sun-glossed bird

Skim rank grass,
Recreate the finale,
Edenic dream shattered,
Tinseled prize become dross.
Across the blurred decades, see
What the boy saw: cot,
Clutter, magician freighting hat
And sleeve with props ... Run blind
Down the midway, spent cocoon
Of childhood left behind
With dust-flung striped balloon ...

Listen ... Only the wind among the weeds ...

SQUIRREL

Dewlight to dusk I watch him
Gather windfall fruit
Preemptive crow and robin
Fail to eat;

Dig down, deposit booty
Midsummer rendered ripe
Deluded that his gaudy
Cache will keep.

Yet how apprise of portent?
In what vernacular
Cry cherries are not acorns,
That apples mar?

TREE DEATH

"No need to mourn a tree," they said.
"It lives, it dies. What more than that?"
But I who'd learned its summer gaud

Of leaf that proffered habitat
To jay and searching wind, who'd slept
And wakened spelled by tree-borne freight

Of light, no less than grove am stripped
Of some essential grace.

TRUCE

Most years it ends in a draw.
Unchecked, ivy threatens the house
Abiding by no other law
Save its own.

Scales chimney, wall, covets sill;
Grown rank, intrudes on glass;
Though pruned, peers in at will
Night, noon.

Wrenched free to no avail
Till clamorous as brass,
Winds ravish, leaf like hail
Flung prone.

LAND BURIAL FOR ONE WHO DROWNED

Your bones are quiet now. There is no tide
To set them rocking like the hulls of ships
That sailed and foundered where the petrel cried,
And lie where black ray lurks, and sea hound slips
Among the rotted spars. Indifferent
To beckoning frond and tentacle, unsung
By squall and flood-voiced shell, you rest now, spent
As spume, inert as starfish shoreward flung.
Here earthed at last, what was the sea's become
Affiliate with stillnesses where web
And inarticulate lichen trace their dumb
Perfections upon stone; the shock and ebb
Of towering tide forgotten where the slow
Unuttered light sheds silences like snow.

JOURNEY

New light quickens;
Up and away ——
Summit that beckons,
The tall, tall day;

Summered and brimmed
With air like glass;
Choired and hymned
By winds and grass.

Such harvest to gather!
Hours ripened by sun
And crystalline weather
Plucked one by one!

No heights to clamber,
The light seen home
Glutted on the amber
Of a honeycomb.

ANT

He strove through windfall petals,
Dragged a crumb of bread
Behind him like a tail.

Paused, spent, to shift his freight,
Resumed, goal coveted
Ant-miles away past white

Mushroom parasol.
What predators ahead
In tuft, in sunburst sprawl

Of dandelion to maim
With sudden spin of thread,
With harsh wasp stratagem?

Detoured, eluding dooms,
Came home at last and fed.

DEAD BEE

It has lost all luster,
Lies among leaves
And windfall burr;

Last seed grain sieved,
Bright bee bread stored
In unnamed hive.

Yet what reward?
Bruised velvet swept
With season's discards;

Whose days were steeped
In roses, trashpiled.

LIMNED ON WATER

Here contour founders. Rarefied
Tree shapes in facsimile
Diffuse as wakened ripples tide
Toward either shore.

All who come to drink are twinned,
Kinship that will not survive
The death of light. Lacewings sunned
Like water hover

As we look down at nether selves,
Finity confirmed; beheld
Briefly filigreed, involved
With gossamer.

BACKYARD FARMER

No summer come, bloom rife
But I remember how
He nurtured backyard sheaf.

An evening farmer slow
With day's fatigue who knelt,
Luxuriated, sowed;

Scanned early corn for fault,
Tied back a row of beans,
Worked on till skies held tilt

Of stars; asleep, dreamt sheen
Of melons round as moons,
Pressed grapes from endless vines.

III

GOLIATHS WITH SIX-GUNS

THE KID AND THE DEVIL

DEVIL *(reading Billy's epitaph from a scroll):*

> Billy the Kid is dead, is dead,
> The thunder stilled within his head,
> His six-gun empty, his bullets spent,
> His murdered soul impenitent.

BILLY:
> In Lincoln County the day I died,
> The prairie rippled like a tide,
>
> And winds from the mountains came to stir
> The purple-berried juniper.
>
> The hills wore light like a diamond collar.
> The air was slick as a silver dollar,
>
> And twangy with sound as a hundred guitars.
> But Hell is a jailhouse without any bars.
>
> The devil is a sheriff with a star on his chest,
> And jail's where a man is lonesomest.
>
> Under the sky I lay alone,
> My threshold dust, my hearth a stone,
>
> And kept no living company.
> But there was a daystar east of me,
>
> And prairie grass beneath my head
> To sing the wind, and make my bed.

DEVIL: The thunder dies, the maze is run;
           There is no sky to hold the sun,
           No prairie grass beneath your head
           To sing the wind, and make your bed.

BILLY: They hawked the tidings up and down
           The sorry length of Lincoln town.

           I heard the wind, and the wind was free,
           But I was pledged to the gallows tree.

           The hills grew tranced to no avail.
           Spring came late to the Lincoln jail,

           Came to hasten the hangmen on,
           Came on the wind like a clarion.

           It witched the field, it spelled the peach,
           It belled the pasqueflower out of reach.

           The birds were loud as a conquering host.
           The hangmen chose the stoutest post.

           The days were a pageant in the sky.
           They planned to build the gallows high,

           A deadwood tree for Lincoln Square.
           They planned the hanging like a county fair.

           But days were tall, and days were wide,
           And Spring was thunder locked inside

           Like a drumfire beat, and a lust grown bigger
           For a horse under me, and a six-gun trigger.

The doomed hours struck. The sky was a riddle.
The days divided down the middle.

The clocks ticked out their deadly rote.
Time was a noose around my throat

To strangle light, to crush me dead.
The thunder shattered in my head.

Over where the courthouse stood,
The carpenters were shaping wood.

The gallows grew. I heard the hammer,
And the saw's insistent clamor.

But the sound of thunder rose
Louder than the hammer blows,

Louder than the striking clocks.
I watched the jailers like a fox.

One was always at my side
To guard me well until I died,

To tend the flesh and feed the bone
Until the gallows claimed its own.

The days were miracles of weather,
And flight a dream of saddle leather,

The sound of wind in the mountain pass,
And piñon trees, and prairie grass,

And Spring like thunder in my head.
I jumped the guard, and shot him dead.

Before the other guard could stir,
Leaping into the corridor,

I shot him too . . . Just the stairway then,
And I was under the sky again.

Plain as plain in the public square,
I mounted a bay horse tethered there,

With never a bullet to roar dissent.
I rode toward the hills, and the thunder went.

They hawked the tidings up and down
The sorry length of Lincoln town.

I heard the wind, and the wind was free,
And I quit claim to the gallows tree.

DEVIL *(intoning)*:

Billy the Kid is dead, is dead,
The thunder stilled within his head,
His six-gun empty, his bullets spent,
His murdered soul impenitent.

BILLY: Whether devil or sheriff—you forget
No prison ever held me yet,

And Hell is a jailhouse without any bars!
DEVIL: To void your days, and quench the stars,

Hell is built contrariwise,
Without horizons, without skies;

Wide yet narrow as a hearse,
Its architecture as diverse

As sin itself; and so designed
To what you most are disinclined;

Subtle and various of shape;
For you a prison you can't escape.

BILLY: Don't mock me, Devil; put to the test,
My six-gun makes an end of jest.

DEVIL: You make a braggart of your gun.
BILLY: An awesome total—twenty-one.

DEVIL: Till Hell has balked your murderous leaning,
It can have but little meaning.

Just shoot a hole through the star on *my* chest!

BILLY *(drawing quickly and attempting to shoot)*:

My gun is empty, and east and west,

Balefires leap and disappear
Athwart the skyless atmosphere.

DEVIL: No drumfire sounds here sun to sun;
No jailers guard you one by one,

Yet should you run, Hell's unwalled space
Would keep you fixed in an embrace

Rigid as death, with each intent
Baffled by Hellish incident.

BILLY: You think to frighten me with tricks
            Magicians keep in conjure-sticks.

            Once at a Lincoln County fair,
            I saw a wizard draw from air

            Dice that glittered, coins and laces,
            A deck of playing cards all aces,

            Who blacked out day with a pinch of snuff,
            And had sleight of hand enough

            To woo the lightning; who could quell
            The storm's great voice, and far outspell

            Your piddling threats and conjurations.
DEVIL: Hell and I have machinations

            Of iniquities compounded,
            Summing darknesses unsounded

            By the cabalistic sages.
            Born of blasphemies and rages,

            Born of anguishes and sighing,
            And the last breaths of the dying,

            Here are sorceries can answer
            Even the wiliest necromancer.

            Once again aim at the star on my chest.
BILLY: Your eyes are strange, and a fiery crest

            Surmounts your brow; and all around,
            Gulfs and crevices abound,

                        [62]

While horsemen ride the air like flame,
And whistling bullets call my name . . .

Yet once before death walked the air
Like flame around me everywhere,

As gunmen, hankering for my hide,
Beckoned with six-guns right outside,

And whistling bullets called my name.
The house around us all aflame,

Besieged without, we made our stand,
McSween with his Bible in his hand,

I with my six-gun, prompting the others,
Charlie and Tom and the Mexican brothers.

McSween was the first to go outside,
Clasping his Bible as he died,

And I, behindhand, after the others,
Charlie and Tom and the Mexican brothers,

Straightened my hat, recocked my gun,
And shot three men as I made my run

To outplay death with the face of flame,
And the whistling bullets that wore my name.

DEVIL: But there was one bullet that did not miss.
Pat Garrett sent you here to this,

Your six-gun useless at your side,
You, not knowing how you died.

BILLY: I could have outgunned him face to face.
It would have been Garrett in my place.

DEVIL: But I was playing Garrett's hand.
Yours was as neat an ambush planned

As any in Hellish history.
Garrett merely moved for me,

Impelled by my satanic cue.
BILLY: Who are you that Hell circles you

With fire to burn away the skies?
DEVIL: Like Hell itself, contrariwise,

I am to each what he hated most,
To every man a different host;

And Hell is many different places—
For you a cell, its twenty paces

To count for all eternity.
BILLY: Once there were winds to sing me free,

And empty skies to hold the sun.
DEVIL: (The thunder dies, the maze is run.)

BILLY: Days had a lilt, and I had a pride
In the deadliest six-gun at my side . . .

It'll take more than a prison cell
To keep me—damned or not—in Hell.

DEVIL: I am sheriff with a star on my chest
           Satanically different than the rest,

           And you are commensurate with dust.
           Rend yourself trying as you must.

           Aim your gun, and balefires burn.
           You have horizons to unlearn,

           And time divided and diurnal.
           Since Hell is endless and infernal,

           Flight shall be your one desire,
           And as you ceaselessly aspire,

           Hell shall crush each new endeavor.
           You are herewith damned forever!

DEVIL *(reading Billy's epitaph)*:

           Billy the Kid is dead, is dead,
           The thunder stilled within his head,
           His six-gun empty, his bullets spent,
           His murdered soul impenitent.

REQUIEM

(For Buffalo Creek—1845-1878)

Let the verse be solemn,
The euphonies muted
And cadenced as dead time.
Unspell dumb
Earth-stopped mouths; refruit dust-routed
Harvests; shape this requiem
To aspiration, to the grey rhyme
Of women wearing homespun, to deed
And sinew, and rhythm of men
Swinging axes; treed
Wilderness hewn,
Become a town . . .
Reflesh the ghost of then.

This town had its Davids who strummed and sang
Psalm tunes and ballads with a western twang;
Goliaths with six-guns who strutted and were downed.
Let the verse be solemn for seven who were drowned,
For hewers and builders and garlanded heads,
For proud men and sober who died in their beds,
For three who were hanged. Let the verse be muted
For those without guile, and those who disputed.

Let each assert his claim!
The now anonymous,
The first who came
With dreams and wagons and the sound
Of jew's-harps—let them speak too.
Like earth and churchyard grass,
This proffered requiem

Disavows no one. They knew
Deer run and salt lick, thicket-crowned
Valley and foothill; venturesome
Acres of beginning,
Upland and level
Furrowed, seed-quickened.
Let the verse echo their long-ago revel,
Their frets, their wooing and winning,
Their outworn grief;
Lost as lost seasons, as arms that beckoned,
Lost in time as year's-end leaf.

This was the hub of town, the halting place
For wayspent stage and buckboard;
Street where bank
And crude emporium abutted rank
Frontier jail. Here seed
And saddle gear were sold, and lace,
And boots and fencing wire and cord;
Here talk exchanged like coin; here winter need
Became addenda on a grocer's list;
Here surge and newness, upgrowth manifest
In visioned scope and stir . . .
Beyond time now, beyond spur
Of hope or season, and besieged by dust.

All vintage throve that year, unmarred
By taint and weather; verdure sleekened
Rise and hollow.
(Let the verse be solemn for husk and shard,
For paths no feet may follow,
And groves no longer fecund.)
Apples swelled with sap,
And young calves balked

At roundup ropes and branding.
Back east they talked
Of railroads and chalked
Junction points and routes upon a map;
Proposing and countermanding
As draftsmen sketched and auditors computed
Disbursements, fees, the most expedient course . . .
About this town, they said:
"Small. Out of the way. Unsuited
For station site. Bypass it just beyond
Those mountains, bearing north instead
Close to the river's source."
The dying started thus with plan and bond
And faraway decree.

Across the country, hammers pounded ties,
Their drumbeat intervals
Evocative of legend, rhythm-wise
As song. Smoke hung upon the light,
Blurring the shattered symmetry
Of newly-blasted hills.
Yet unaware
Of augured change and ban,
This town held stillnesses and bright
Unsullied air . . .
But then the exodus began,
The laden wagons, the slow arduous haul,
Tradesmen first, and tall
Restless cowhands; smith,
Saddlemaker, farmer and drone.
Unfleshed as bone,
The town died, became a myth,
A dream in retrospect, wraith and host
To dust.

IV

GIRL OF SUMER

GIRL OF SUMER

(Sumerian royalty were buried in stone tombs with
men and women of rank in orderly rows beside them.
The latter were evidently interred alive since their re-
mains showed no signs of violence. A rolled-up silver
headband was found near one young girl. Perhaps she
had been late dressing for the ceremony, and put it in
her pocket with the intention of putting it on later, but
forgot.)

Girl of Sumer robed for doom,
The silver fillet at your feet,
Did you go willing to the tomb?

Your thin arms braceleted for whom?
Your stiff-dressed hair, your mouth made sweet,
Girl of Sumer robed for doom?

"The queen is dead," they cried. "Let plume
And purple pennant deck the street!"
Did you go willing to the tomb?

Rouged, trailing ribbons and perfume,
What apprehensions kept discreet,
Girl of Sumer robed for doom?

All games done never to resume,
The gilded ritual complete,
Did you go willing to the tomb?

Or loath to leave your childhood room,
What household gods did you entreat,
Girl of Sumer robed for doom?
Did you go willing to the tomb?

INDIAN MADONNA, GUADALUPE, MEXICO

No Renaissance Madonna this brown girl
With Indian berry eyes and nightfall hair,
Devoid of cloak and aureole; dark swirl
Of skirt, of artless bodice, her arms bare,
Her plow-bred hands replete with flowers. Elect,
She stands bemused, unwitting flesh endowed
With portent; poised in time, not yet bedecked
With epic grief or glory, not yet proud.
Turned inward, strangely diffident who plied
Ancestral village tasks, and now perceives
Within herself transcendence like a tide;
This bearer of water, gatherer of sheaves,
Apprised, hears advent like a distant drum
Of grace, of paean fraught with martyrdom.

APPLE IN THE HAND

No dream can parallel the sun,
Nor dreamlit pedagogy teach
The nooning day's phenomenon,
The curvate structure of a peach;

Nor sleep-shaped fancies fabricate
A climate oak trees understand;
No nightshade Eden may equate
The apple cherished in the hand.

THE MAD LIBRARIAN

How tall is light that stretches to the sun
Unwalled and free?
Forgotten now in wherefores and in whys.
This room makes finite all infinity,
Squaring the circle of each day undone,
And shutting out the pageant of the skies.
Lost, forever lost to me
The black-winged flight of clouds across the moon.
Locked in the mind,
The darkness merges with the afternoon,
Today with yesterday, before with soon;
Since walls are blind,
I cannot know how broad horizons are,
Or how the light is filtered from a star,
How time is hung in space and days divide.
My world is eight feet tall and eight feet wide.

I am lovely, I am lovely,
And my hair's the silken wing
Of a blackbird fluttering.
I am Lydia, Lydia Pritchett, I am lovely
And my name is like a bonnet,
Velvet crowned, with feathers on it—
I am lovely in my bonnet
And my hair's a blackbird's wing.
But who is that keeps muttering?
Books? What books? There are no books here.
"Yes, sir, B shelf to the right."
(Your arms an engulfing hemisphere
To cradle my delight!)

And you, and you,
And you, and you,
Consult the file
For love's clear cue,
And dream hymeneal dreams the while
Of unlearned lips and shaken hair
Learned in a consummating night.
"Yes, sir, B shelf to the right."
(Within your arms I swoon and quiver,
Then awaken with a shiver.)
There are no books, there are no dreams;
        these crushing walls are bare.

BEDFELLOWS

Caught in its own web,
Betrayed by drift of season,
Spider, prey hobnob;

Indifferent to spun
Gossamer of shared
Frost-lustred shroud. Each one

Neat-noosed, abruptly paired,
What matter which beguiled
With fatal lace, which snared?

Together domiciled,
Captor, moth, grace blown,
Equated. Helen felled,
Dead as any crone.

DÉJÀ VU

Departing, I look back
Who cannot leave a place
I've known; mourn bric-a-brac

And eaves, the windowed tree
That brought its seasons close.
For such affinity,

Lot's wife was judged at fault.
Will my flesh turn to salt?

DEATH OF AN ACTRESS

This scene is unrehearsed,
No script, no prompter's cue;
A one night stand, a first

For her without review
Or curtain call. She lies
Stripped of heroics who

Had postured in disguise
The death of queens, had wrung
With Juliet's demise

In rich iambics flung
Like minted coins. Devoid
Of spotlight, exits: tongue,

Hands freighted, all things said,
All her mantles shed.

AUBADE

This is waking: sortilege
And breadth of light; the anchorage

Of morning moored upon a leaf,
Moon-tide breasted, nightmare reef

Outrun; anew the endless riddle
Of day divided in the middle,

Measured in sequence. Waking is this:
Time's reaffirmed hypothesis

Of laws diurnal that ordain
The cycle's end, begun again.

SKATING RINK — ROCKEFELLER CENTER

"I used to skate," he said. Old eyes appraised
This fledgling skater, that. "But there were woods
Between the house and pond, spent leaves, snow bruised

By hasty footsteps; each of us pursued,
Pursuer eager to be first. No blare
Of horns. Just easy winter sounds: the treed

Sough of wind, attendant icefall rare
As glass . . . But now I watch all afternoon.
We used to bandy tricks, outrace, outdare

Each other by the hour until the sun
Attained horizon. Shadows saw us home."
Hunched down, grew still, his coat a great cocoon.

I said: "Bystanders—that's what we become."
He shrugged. Then: "Gleaners battened on a crumb."

STROKE VICTIM

Daily fed, beguiled
With colored pills and flowers,
Sits trussed up like a child.
Her tongue betrays her.
Unreconciled,
Her thoughts walk, bob
In dance as limbs cannot.

Visitors
Dissemble, are glib.
Nurses hover
Cool as cream.

Daylong her eyes implore,
Pray, scream
In anguished polyglot.

No one hears.

QUARREL

Stripped of love's raiment, I am all undone;
Of sense, of substance, beggared: palpably
Defined in ice, your silence, and in stone,
Numbing and crushing me.

Divided hence, once coalesced and kin.
Now withered beneath the frost of your disdain,
Possessed of no armor save this mortal skin,
I am all but slain.

Plunged down and down, forever the abysm,
Way and beyond till I, your planetoid,
Flung from your orbit in anger's cataclysm
Am utterly destroyed.

HOSPITAL VOLUNTEER

I am brisk as usual.
I bring a mug of milk.
Your eyes inspect the wall.

(Inert . . . so little bulk
Beneath the sheet.) I coax
A bit, pretend to sulk.

"A magazine?" I fix
The cover come awry.
Your silence builds like blocks.

I smooth your bed. I play
It cool. (On whose behalf?)
Affect hyperbole—

We each taste chaff.

NOAH AND MRS. EPSTEIN

For my grandmother to whom the
patriarchs were as contemporane-
ous as her newspaper.

Affiliate to her
As frequent friend and neighbor

Who come for fruit and tea,
Discuss catastrophe,

His presence looms, great beard
And God-loved girth restored

To being; and what he told
His frightened kin assailed

By doubt of doomsday wrath
And grace, flood's aftermath,

Evokes in his behalf
Awe, pride, grief.

SUICIDE

For Alex who liked to feed the birds.

I give them bread,
My sparrows
Who hear winter
In the changing light.

My thoughts toll out
Like great bronze bells,
But pavements,
Intent on footfalls,
Pay no heed.

Look up and up.
I shall launch my flight
From the rooftop,
Arms outspread
Like air-spent wings.

My sparrows
Who wear no shoes,
And do not fear the snow,
Will listen.

SECOND CHANCE

Strange how they come in dream,
Wear ample flesh, move, talk
As I would have them, limb

And bearing tall, the shock
Of death forgotten. Spelled,
This dreamer ruled by clock

And timeless dead to bold
New affinity.
At last no thought withheld,

Old guilts that burdened me
Here given tongue, outworn.
Thus purged, self, kin set free,

I seek to bind, am torn—
Wake, wind a distant horn.

UNQUIET FLESH

To Heloise, the nun.

Her vows are garments of escape
To exorcise with inward flight
That passion bright as a lantern shape
Describing light.

Her thoughts with orisons enmesh;
Her Aves counter love and hate.
To stifle her unquiet flesh,
She counts the convent plate.

Though fancy dulls with pieties,
And sweet memorials of lust
Die hourly, ground by prayerful knees
Into the shriving dust,

Of fasts and penances are bred
Those dreams, incontinently starred
That mock her in her convent bed
With shades of Abelard.

THE WINDING SHEET

(We are told in the Odyssey that Penelope, the wife of
Odysseus, never stopped hoping for his return. She kept
her brutish suitors at bay by asking permission to finish
the winding sheet she was preparing for Laertes, the
father of Odysseus so that he would not go unshrouded
when he died. She prolonged this task by undoing at
night what she had woven during the day.)

This cloth you weave, Penelope
Is textured warp and woof
Of decades restive as the sea
You hourly scan, reproof

And love set counter, thought and weft
Enlaced in loomed deceit;
Hope wound like thread; mind, hands grown deft:
Unravel, plait, repeat.

While suitors rage, and gods are dumb,
You pattern from despair
Odysseus' footfalls like a drum
Jarring the palace stair.

AFTER THE ODYSSEY

Are you content, Odysseus, warrior, wit
To count your aging days before the fire
Concerned with shepherd's quarrel, rural writ
Defining law and levy;

Your bow unstrung, great shield upon the wall
While Troy and Circe, battle fought and won
Are phrased to legend in your banquet hall
Amidst libation, revel, yawn;

Or do you hunger when you lie beside
Your good grey wife for brazen panoply,
And hear like music restive as the tide
Dream-voiced Nausicaa by the sounding sea?

HELEN OF TROY
TWENTY YEARS LATER

Queen and wife of Menelaus,
Do your thoughts flicker
Like your fingers as you spin,
And chide the Spartan girls who bicker
Over household chores?
What echoes storm the palace corridors
As you pour the banquet wine,
As the harper plays,
As you bind up your radiant hair?
Unbidden, do battle trumpets blare,
Paris, Hector, tall Achilles come
To thrust, to die
Again, again, again?

FAIRY TALE

The prince in frog disguise
Perched noon-lulled upon ledge
Blinks languid eyes, surveys

His rank domain; cortege
But gnat and dragonfly
That hover, skirting sedge

And pondscape mimicry
Of sky. Lost self yet bound
In strange identity,

He outwaits light. Uncrowned,
No perfect princess come,
He plunges down past frond

And lily, sleeps where dumb
Tendrils root in slime.

STONEHENGE

(whose axis points toward the
sunrise on June 21, the longest
day of the year.)

These pillars measure seasons
By arcane arithmetic
Their hewers knew in their bones;

Men in shaggy skins
Who never dreamed the wheel
Yet calendared the sun
Which marked the solstice.

Did they chant, kneel,
Perform fecund rite
When midsummer flared with yield

Or redden altar stone
To counter storm, siege,
Winter's wolfscape night?

LAST STOP

Atop the mounded trash
Noisome with its lush
Compost of scraps, bones
And old leaves, a pair
Of glasses, history unknown;

Their borrowed light shocked
To blindness, nosepiece tricked
To flesh-taught contour, spent
Of warmth, awry.
What seas, what firmament

Restored to hue, star,
Breadth by curvature
Of lens? What purblind eyes
Apprised of dewed
Grassblade symmetries?

No hands that fold them neat
And cherished to await
Dawn, they craze and weather
Unmourned as stones
Where gulls and rodents gather.

A LACK OF THUNDER

The mirror in your room
Does not recall your face.
The walls continue dumb.

Untroubled by reproof,
Clock hands maintain their pace.
Your chair stands back, aloof.

Beset I grope for sign
That loss has visited.
Daylong dust motes drift down,

Are ultimate, lay claim
To unencumbered bed,
And nothing speaks your name.